STEP GENTLY IN THE WORLD

STEP GENTLY
IN THE WORLD

Resources for Holy Week

Sally Foster-Fulton

wild goose
publications www.**ionabooks**.com

Overseas distribution
Australia: Willow Connection Pty Ltd, Unit 4A, 3-9 Kenneth Road,
Manly Vale, NSW 2093
New Zealand: Pleroma, Higginson Street, Otane 4170, Central Hawkes Bay
Canada: Novalis/Bayard Publishing & Distribution, 10 Lower Spadina Ave.,
Suite 400, Toronto, Ontario M5V 2Z2

Printed by Bell & Bain, Thornliebank, Glasgow

CONTENTS

INTRODUCTION

Holy Week: the space to consider where the journey with Jesus might lead us …

However, too often we yield to the temptation of waving our palm branches in the air one Sunday, rolling Easter eggs down the hill the next, smiling 'He is risen' at each other, while not allowing ourselves to enter the story.

The story is ours and we are called to walk the way with Jesus, learning the lessons of Holy Week again and rediscovering the daunting freedom of resurrection.

Thanks to my family for helping me find the space to write this book, especially my dad, who was the ultimate storyteller and beacon.

Sally Foster-Fulton

PALM SUNDAY

THERE ARE ALWAYS TWO PARADES

(Reflection at Faslane nuclear weapons base)

Tomorrow is Palm Sunday – the day children wave their palm branches and parade down the aisles to 'Hosanna, Loud Hosanna'. The day the church remembers Jesus' triumphal entry into Jerusalem. The beginning of a Holy Week that seemingly ended in tears, but lives on. Tomorrow is Palm Sunday, and today, as we gather together here to pray and protest, we remember that ancient parade for peace down the Mount of Olives.

There have been a lot of parades since then … marches for equality and justice: the Salt March led by Gandhi in India, the march on Washington led by Martin Luther King, the protest in Tiananmen Square … and so many more.

Did you know that there were two parades that day? We should know it – the first people who heard this story would have certainly known it, every single one of them – Jesus' little ragtag procession would have been a blip on the screen compared to what was going on on the other side of town.[1]

On the other side of town, Pontius Pilate was entering Jerusalem – coming in from the coast with 600 foot-soldiers, horses, armour, banners and flags and standards bearing great carved golden eagles (the symbol of Roman authority), beating drums, the cadence of heavy foot-fall … Jerusalem during Passover would have been teeming with Jewish pilgrims and been a hotbed of tension – and Rome wanted Israel to be in no doubt about who was in charge. Can you imagine it? And the cheers would have been eerily similar to the ones we think of when we remember Palm Sunday: Caesar was Rome's 'Prince of Peace'; Caesar was Rome's 'Son of God', and Pontius Pilate was his representative.

And then came Jesus, down the Mount of Olives on a donkey: on an agricultural 'tool', not a war machine. The imagery couldn't have been clearer: 'I am for peace!' This triumphal entry was a send-up, a take-the-mickey parody of Pilate's grand procession – a mockery of it. It wasn't an accident either: it was a staged demonstration.

So we here today follow in a long line of holy protests. Jesus' disciples claimed that real power and authority sat with peace: the 'Son of God' and 'Prince of Peace'. And so do we.

'So what?' some might say. 'So what if there were two parades – what does that matter?'

Well, I think it matters, because there are always two parades, aren't there? … And we have to decide which one we'll join.

When we choose to forgive – or not … we walk a certain way.

When we choose what we'll do with our money, our energy, our love … we walk a certain way.

When we gather in the cold on the Saturday before Palm Sunday, standing in the footsteps of those who have protested for peace, justice, freedom and no nuclear weapons, we are choosing which parade we are joining …

There are always two parades in town … and the ever-present question is: *'Which one will you join?'* …

---

[1] See *The Last Week,* by Marcus J. Borg and John Dominic Crossan, HarperCollins

THROUGH THE HOSANNAS

(Opening responses)

Through the hosannas and the waving palms, the singing and the joy,
come, and walk the road with Christ.

HOSANNA! BLESSED IS HE WHO COMES IN THE NAME OF THE LORD.
WE WILL WALK WITH HIM.

Through the betrayal and the denial, the shouting and the sorrow,
come, and walk the road with Christ.

BEHOLD, THE LAMB OF GOD,
WHO TAKES AWAY THE SINS OF THE WORLD.
WE WILL WALK WITH HIM.

Through the waving palms and the passion, the prayers and the pain,
come, and walk the road with Him.

WE WILL WALK WITH HIM.
WE WILL NOT LEAVE HIM NOW.
HOSANNA! BLESSED IS HE WHO COMES IN THE NAME OF THE LORD.

RIDE ON

Voice one:

Christ, you rode on: through the riotous cheers and the menacing uneasy whispers ... you rode on towards a place they could not imagine, and you asked them to follow ... And Christ – it's frightening ... because all these centuries later, you ask the same thing: *'Stay with me'* ... *'Follow me.'* You keep asking us to get up – to follow your path – to change our ways, our direction, our way of thinking.

Voice two:

But all too often, we stage a sit-down strike. All too often, instead of following and staying with you, we choose to stay put – to stick close to what's familiar – to surround ourselves with our own kind ... to relax in our comfort zones ... During this most holy week, help us to change direction ... Help us to take up our lives and walk with you and for others.

Voice one:

Christ, you keep asking us to be still: to listen for your voice, to think before we act or speak, to keep our feet firmly on the ground so they have a chance of staying out of our mouths.

Voice two:

But all too often, Lord, we go racing on ahead – blithely ignoring your call for calm. Far too often, instead of being still and abiding in you, we go it alone, and end up with a lot of backtracking to do ... During this most holy time, help us to stay near you ... to consider our journey so that we walk with you and for others.

Voice one:

God, you keep asking us to go the extra mile – to walk with others, to share our provisions, to veer off and visit the prisoner or feed the hungry, to carry your cross …

Voice two:

But all too often, Lord, we give up halfway, and run off, or amble away, or do an impressive sidestep … During this most holy time, help us to keep dancing and limping on, that our steps may accompany yours and be for others.

Voice one:

Christ, as you ride on through the riotous cheers and the menacing uneasy whispers … as you ride on towards a place we cannot imagine, help us to stay with you, help us to follow … For we are the body that has come after you … we are the answer to your prayers. Idle watchers would call that foolish; hesitant wavers would call that frightening … but we, gathered here today, call that a blessing.

Voice two:

Let us pray …

For all the beauty you have given us,
for the peace that has come at great cost,
for your promise to stay with us forever,
even through our wanderings,
Christ of mercy, we thank you.

We are the body that has come after you:
we are the answer to your prayers.
When you walked this earth with us,
you healed the sick,
held the hurting,
made folk whole:
you prayed that God's will would be done.

Today, as we gather here,
we gather also in our hearts
all those who are hurt and need healing,
your broken ones who yearn for wholeness ...
and we pray to you for the strength to help them,
for we are the body that has come after,
and we pray that we may be
the answer to your prayers.
Amen

Voice one:

So what will it be?

Voice two:

What indeed?

TO TELL THE TRUTH

A Palm Sunday service

This is based on the game show To Tell The Truth. *Three contestants enter from the chapter house/vestry and line up. Canned music to start the show.*

Game show host:

Good evening and welcome to *To Tell the Truth* – the game show where three contestants try to convince you and our panel of judges that they are the *real deal*. Of course, only one of them can be – so who is telling the truth?

First, let's meet our panel of judges: *(e.g. the minister, a Sunday-school teacher, an RMPS teacher, depending on your local situation; use the people's real names throughout).*

OK, now let's meet our contestants:

Number 1, what is your name?

Jesus 1:

My name is Jesus Christ.

Game show host:

Number 2, what is your name?

Jesus 2:

My name is Jesus Christ.

Game show host:

Number 3, what is your name?

Jesus 3:

My name is Jesus Christ.

Game show host:

Now, panellists, open your envelopes and read along as I share the following statement:

I, Jesus Christ, aka Jesus of Nazareth, the Son of Man, the Son of God, the son of David, the Vine, the Bread of life, the King of kings, the Messiah – you get the message – *was born over two thousand years ago in Bethlehem in Judea, so the story goes. I grew up in Nazareth, the eldest son of the Virgin Mary and Joseph, a local carpenter. Although there were mysterious stories told about my birth, nothing much happened until I was about thirty. Then, after I was baptised by my cousin John in the River Jordan, I found God (or God found me), and then I preached my way across Israel, until I ran into trouble in Jerusalem and was executed by the Roman government. After my death, there were reports that I was resurrected, and it is said that my life continues to influence things even today. My best friends, after getting off to a bit of a rocky start, continued to teach and share my message, and now there are over two billion people in the world who claim to follow me. They are called Christians and although they all stake a claim on me, they often have trouble agreeing with each other. Signed ... Jesus Christ.*

Game show host:

OK, not an easy one. Could we have a question from our first panellist to get us started?

Panellist 1:

Yes, Jesuses – you used a lot of different names to describe yourself in that statement and in your life. Which one, or ones, really describes you?

Jesus 1 (wimpy, wet, sitting on the fence):

Well, they're all special to me, and I wouldn't want to upset the apple cart by taking a stand or anything. But if I were pushed, ones like 'holy' and 'beloved' and 'Lamb' are nice. Don't you think?

Panellist 1:

Er, yes ... Number 2?

Jesus 2 (Military 'GI' Jesus):

Well, not to boast, but I've been called the King of kings, the Lord Jesus Christ, the Great Lion of the tribe of Judah ... Folk would do well to remember what my cousin said about me coming with a winnowing fork in my hand. It was also said somewhere that I did not come to bring peace, but the sword – know what I mean? Forget Judge Judy – meet Judge Jesus.

Panellist 1:

Yes, sir! ... Number 3?

Jesus 3 (Jesus the Peacemaker):

Hi. They have called me the 'Son of God'. And it is written *'Blessed are the peacemakers, for they will be called sons of God.'* To my friend Jesus Number 2, all I can say is that: *'All who draw the sword, will die by the sword.'* Brave are the folk who believe in forgiveness: the ones who can practise it over and over again. Many people tried to make me into their own version of a Messiah. I never called myself a king, and I got into a lot of trouble for taking a stand. If I'm the Son of God, then I'm your brother, and that'll do for me.

(Buzzer goes.)

Game show host:

Thank you Jesuses. OK, Panellist Number 2, do you have a question?

Panellist 2:

Yes. Jesus Number One, in Sunday school we tell lots of stories to the children – mostly ones about you. Do you have a favourite?

Jesus 1:

Well, they're all special to me, and I wouldn't want to upset the apple cart by taking a stand or anything. But if I were pushed, the ones I especially like are the ones about when I was born – the angels singing and the star shining, the wise men coming to visit and bringing those lovely gifts … the little drummer boy and the elves.

Panellist 2:

Um, I don't remember any elves.

Jesus 1:

Sorry, I misremembered.

Panellist 2:

Number 2?

Jesus 2 (looks disdainfully at Jesus 1):

There are so *many* cool stories – the action ones sum me up: walking on the water, driving out demons – and those pesky money-changers in the Temple – they didn't have a chance! And I like the ones in Revelation about when I come back and really clean up! But maybe those aren't appropriate for the wee ones.

Panellist 2:

Wow! ... Number 3?

Jesus 3:

Stories are meant to tell you something else entirely: if they're just saying what happened, then fine, but there's not much mileage in that. The stories I like best are the ones that point to what I'm about and what God's about. I love the ones where people are fed, because God loves the hungry. I love the ones about forgiveness, because God is all over that. I love the ones where the outcast or the stranger gets to be the hero – because the kingdom of God turns what we expect on its head! And I love a good old-fashioned love story, don't you?

Panellist 2 (blushes a wee bit):

Yeah, I do.

(Buzzer goes.)

Game show host:

OK, last panellist … What's your question?

Panellist 3:

Jesuses, nice to meet you. I've heard an awful lot about you. I teach Religious, Moral and Philosophical Studies, so I'm involved with getting young people to engage with many different faiths and ideas. In the New Testament it says: *No one comes to God except by you.* What do you say about that? … Number 2?

Jesus 2:

Hell, yeah! That's what I say. You've gotta watch out for those false prophets in sheep's clothing – and remember, if you're not with me, you're against me! *'I am the Way'* – so it's 'my Way or the highway'.

Panellist 3:

Hmmm … Number 1?

Jesus 1:

Well, you're all special to me, and I wouldn't want to upset the apple cart by taking a stand or anything – so don't push me on this. Just remember to come to church and pledge your money and keep things ticking over the way they are. OK? … Please? …

Panellist 2:

Hmmm … Number 3?

Jesus 3:

Jesus Number 2, the quote you're using comes from the Gospel of John, and there are so many different ways to understand it. It's interesting, but in the quote you used: *'I am the way, the truth and the life. No one comes to God except by me'*, there is a reference to 'I am'. 'I am' is the only name God ever gives to God's self: Yahweh: *I am who I am, I was who I was, I will be who I will be*: so plenty of room for different understandings, different paths and people. In those stories Panellist 2 asked about earlier, if you look closely: I never closed a door, never said no to someone in need, never forced my way. And at the end of that bit in the Gospel of John, it is peace that I leave with you …

Panellist 2:

Hmm.

Game show host:

OK, panellists – now make your judgements, and no conferring. Write them down and turn them in … *(Panellists consider, and hand in their cards.)*

And now …… will the real Jesus Christ please step forward? ……

(All three Jesuses look at each other, fake stepping forward and then shrug … then turn together and return to the chapter house/vestry.)

Worship leader:

Who is the real Jesus? That really depends on you, doesn't it? … Because you embody him. Whoever he is will live on in you and me, so – will the real Jesus Christ please step forward? … Let us worship God.

Song: 'Lord, make us servants of your peace' (CH4 527)

Reading: Luke 19:28–40:

Voice 1:

… He went on ahead, going up to Jerusalem. When he had come near Beth-phage and Bethany, at the place called the Mount of Olives, he sent two of the disciples, saying,

Voice 2:

'Go into the village ahead of you, and as you enter it you will find tied there a colt that has never been ridden. Untie it and bring it here. If anyone asks you, "Why are you untying it?" just say this, "The Lord needs it".'

Voice 1:

So those who were sent departed and found it as he had told them. As they were untying the colt, its owners asked them,

Voice 3:

'Why are you untying the colt?'

Voice 4:

They said, 'The Lord needs it.'

Voice 1:

Then they brought it to Jesus; and after throwing their cloaks on the colt, they set Jesus on it. As he rode along, people kept spreading their cloaks on the road. As he was now approaching the path down from the Mount of Olives, the whole multitude of the disciples began to praise God joyfully with a loud voice for all the deeds of power that they had seen, saying,

Voices 3 and 4:

'Blessed is the king who comes in the name of the Lord! Peace in heaven, and glory in the highest heaven!'

Voice 1:

Some of the Pharisees in the crowd said to him,

Voices 3 and 4:

'Teacher, order your disciples to stop.'

Voice 1:

He answered,

Voice 2:

'I tell you, if these were silent, the stones would shout out.'

Song: 'Ride on, ride on, the time is right' (CH4 370)

The worship leader picks up a stone and holds it up:

Leader:

What would the stones shout out? ... What would they say about this man riding along the road? They've had a chequered history after all: they've been used to build up, of course – walls, homes, cities, temples … Commandments were etched on them. They've been shaped and used as tools: to harvest, to mend …

But they've also been thrown at unchaste women and disobedient children. Stones would have pelted a woman caught in adultery, but Jesus spoke first and then no one felt self-righteous enough to throw the first one; so they were dropped on to the road, into the sand.

Stones have made fine weapons – flung from slings, tipping arrows and topping spears.

So, would they echo holy hallelujahs … or scream out for war?

Tonight is the night of the choice: which parade will we join, which force? Across the city, Rome marches – coming into Jerusalem like a violent wave. The Festival is beginning, and whenever people gather, power makes a show. But here, on this path down from the Mount of Olives, is Jesus, making another stand, with his own show. He chooses peace, and will not turn from the way when life gets frightening and death is imminent.

Who knows what the stones will shout … those ancient creations with their chequered past.

What about you? What do you say? What parade will your feet join? Who is your real Jesus? …

We are going to listen to some music now: a time to think before you move; a time to choose, if you can, which path you'll follow …

After the music, you will be invited to come to the centre of the church, where some stones have been scattered. Pick one up and take it back to your seat. You'll be given more instructions after.

Music: time for reflection

Action: folk come and pick up a stone

Meditation:

Leader:

Hold your stone and look at it: ancient creation with its chequered past …

Think of yourself – newer creation – also home to moments of beauty and glimpses of glory; also keeper of times of trouble and turbulence – things you'd rather not dwell on.

Sit with your stone and hear it speak …

Moment of silence

Voice 1:

Listen now to the prayer of the stone:

You stepped gently on the earth, O Christ of all;
and you treat gently all those who come your way.
Turn us into tools that transform,
not weapons that wear and warp,
diminish and destroy.
We lie vulnerable in the hands of your children.
May they hold peace.

Response: verse 1 of 'Put peace into each other's hands' (CH4 659), sung by a small choir

Voice 2:

(Prayer of the stone continued):

You spoke and lived generously on the earth, O Christ of all.
You taught and healed
and united all those who came your way.
Build us into good things, lasting things –
things that help,
not things that hurt.
May we be bridges that bring people together,
not barriers that stand in the way.
May we be buildings that shelter
and homes that keep hearts safe.
We lie vulnerable in the hands of your children.
May they hold peace.

Response: 'Put peace into each other's hands' (verse 1)

Leader:

Step gently as you leave. Tonight is the start of Holy Week.

In the crossing is the beginnings of a cairn. If you'd like to leave your stone there, as a symbol of God's constant presence in our chequered past, present and future, then say a silent prayer for peace and lay it down as you leave.

If instead you'd like to keep the stone, then that's fine too.

We sing together 'Night has fallen' (CH4 222).

Blessing:

Go in peace.
Remain in peace.
Return in peace.
Amen

Message at the cairn:

Step gently in the world. This is Holy Week.

On Palm Sunday, a vigil for peace was held in the church. These stones represent the prayers said by those who gathered here.

We invite you to take part by offering your own prayer for peace, by placing a stone on the cairn.

(Leave a supply of stones for pilgrims.)

MONDAY
OF HOLY WEEK

LOVE WASTEFULLY
AND SAVE THE WORLD

(On John 12:1–8, Jesus anointed at Bethany)

For this service you will need spikenard, or another essential oil.

Call to worship:

Leader:

Please join hands a moment ...

Pause

Feel the strength of a touch, the intimacy of contact, the warmth and uniqueness of each human being ...

And as you let go, realise that the feeling remains and the memory comforts. Listen to the truth:

Voice 1:

Love lingers, hope holds, peace perseveres long after the lover and the hoper and the peacemaker are gone.

Voice 2:

For no matter what separates you – fear, despair, anger, injustice, death itself – nothing is stronger than love. Nothing on earth or beyond can conquer it or make it cower.

Voice 1:

Love lingers, hope holds, peace perseveres long after the lover and the hoper and the peacemaker are gone.

Voice 2:

Do not miss your moment to join with the ones whose lives have proved this to be true. When your moment comes, pour out your love with utter abandon.

Voice 1:

And you will gain everything.

Prayer:

God, touch me:

when talking is too tiresome
and conversation has dried up and blown away.

Hold me:

when hell has found its way to earth
and surrounds me.
Then being held may be the only way
to bring any healing there is to be had.

Embrace me:

when every effort has been made to rectify the situation,
but it is too far gone and the end must come.
I may not respond or even reach out in return,
but I will know you are there.

God, we say this to you on a night when we remember
that you have said it to us.
Amen

Song: 'Love is the touch' (from *One Is the Body*)

Leader:

Tonight we go back to before the palm branches are waved and the coats
are thrown cavalierly to the ground and the alleluias are sung to the skies.

Tonight, we sit in a house with his friends and bear witness to a unique love
story. The Gospel of John places this story before any other of this holy
week. It acts as a foreshadowing – Mary, an unlikely role model. And I like
it here because it comforts me that someone comforted him before the
huge struggle began. Listen for the Word of God:

Bible reading: John 12:1–8

Heaven sent (a meditation):

She'd used spikenard, a whole pound of it ... it wouldn't have just filled the
room, or even the house – the scent would have clung to all of those
present – it would have hung on their clothes, it would have settled in their
hair, it would have permeated and overwhelmed their senses. That much
pure essential oil would have been so powerful, you would have almost

tasted it. And it wouldn't have dissipated quickly or easily, but would have remained.

Mary's hair would have held that fragrance for a long time – after he was gone, the memory would stay with her, more alive because her sense of smell would have brought it flooding back. And so every time she moved or walked, tossed in her sleep or put her head in her hands, she would have been reminded of him – of what he had meant to her, done for her – what she had done for him.

Some had told her that her extravagant act had been wasteful, but she didn't agree. I mean, really, how can you waste love?

I wonder how long the scent stayed with him – when they waved their palm branches in the air, did the fragrance waft through the crowds, did it stir some deep-seated emotion in them? Would they have understood its significance? And would he have felt a bit more determined because of this lingering anointment?

Before the disruption started in earnest, when his soul was troubled, did it ease him? I am certain that it hung in the air in the upper room as the feet were washed and the supper eaten.

And then, when the trouble came so rapidly and his friends fell away and there was betrayal and denial, I wonder if he was comforted ... upheld ... affirmed by the fragrance that still surrounded, embraced him. When he was marched and dragged all over Jerusalem, I wonder if the oil still soothed his feet. When they drove the nails in, did the sedative effects calm him, the scent reassure him. And at what everyone else thought was the very end, I wonder if he looked down and saw her face, remembered her gesture when the breeze sent the aroma to him.

She'd used spikenard, a whole pound of it ... it wouldn't have just filled the room or even the house on the night he was anointed – the scent would have clung to all of those present – it would have hung on their clothes, it would have settled in their hair, it would have permeated and overwhelmed their senses. That much pure essential oil would have been so powerful, you would have almost tasted it. And it wouldn't have dissipated quickly or easily, but would have remained.

Some had told her that her extravagant act had been wasteful, but she didn't agree – neither did he. I mean, really, how can you waste love?

Song: 'Said Judas to Mary' (duet) (by Sydney Carter)

Leader:

We have been told what love is: it is patient and kind, it rejoices in the truth, it bears all things, believes all things, hopes all things, endures all things. Love never ends. And in this story, we have been told that, really, it cannot be wasted.

Who knows how long your gifts of love, no matter how costly, will cling and linger, comfort and reassure. Love does not dissipate quickly or easily, but remains. Think of those who gifted you with love – how those gifts have held you! Those are the faces you still see, the voices you still hear, the touches you can still feel long after they have gone. Those are the times in your life that do not dissipate easily or quickly, because they are so powerful. We need to remember this story of Mary, who did not hold back her gift, but poured it out with abandon.

I think we need to remember this story:

when we decide about how we will spend our money;
when we think about how what we have and what we do
impacts on the folk we share life and the planet with.

I think we need to remember this story:

when we talk to our children;
and when we argue with our lovers;
and when we decide about how we will spend – yes spend! –
the time God has given us here on this earth …

She used spikenard, a whole pound of it … it wouldn't have just filled the room or even the house – the scent would have clung to all of those present – it would have hung on their clothes, it would have settled in their hair, it would have permeated and overwhelmed their senses. That much pure essential oil would have been so powerful, you would have almost tasted it. And it wouldn't have dissipated quickly or easily, but would have remained.

Some had told her that her extravagant act had been wasteful, but she didn't agree – neither did he. I mean, really, how can you waste love? Go out and use it – all you have – it won't dissipate easily or quickly – it will remain with those you have loved.

Song: 'Lo, I am with you' (from *There Is One Among Us*)

Introduction to symbolic action:

Leader:

Mary used spikenard, a whole pound of it. It would have clung to all of those present – hung on their clothes, settled in their hair, permeated and overwhelmed their senses. And it wouldn't have dissipated quickly or easily, but would have remained.

As we sing the song of commitment, please come forward and receive a blessing and have the sign of the cross placed on your palm. We too will use spikenard. Afterwards, please return to your seat for the benediction.

Action: (during the singing of 'In love you summon, in love I follow', from *There Is One Among Us*)

Benediction:

Go out:
love wastefully and save the world.

Go out:
live foolishly and be wise.

Go out:
you cannot love too much.

Amen

Sally Foster-Fulton, with Ruth Burgess

TUESDAY
OF HOLY WEEK

THIS IS THE HOUSE OF GOD

Music for reflection (mood: calm building to a nervous tension …)

Call to worship:

Tonight he gets mad – angry, livid, furious, ticked off and set off – more than annoyed. Some would say he lost it! What he saw was one step too far, as far as he was concerned. But why? … On this Holy Tuesday, Jesus gets mad.

Song: 'I rejoiced when I heard them say' (CH4 83)

Reading: Mark 11:15–19

During or just after the reading 'Jesus' comes striding up the aisle of the church to the crossing and very noisily overturns a table with piles of coins set upon it (use about 20 quid worth of new pennies). He yells: 'My father's house shall be called a house of prayer for all the nations – but you have made it a den of thieves!', and strides out. Make this dramatic and disturbing. Practise it.

Song: 'Inspired by love and anger' (CH4 253)

Meditation:

I really don't know what the problem was. I think the stress was finally get-ting to him and he overreacted. I mean, all this was happening in the Court of the Gentiles – the place where anyone could go to pray, not just the High Priests or peon-priests, not just the Jewish men or even women – but anyone! So what was the big deal? It's not like they were selling doves in the choirs, or trading unfairly from the nave … it was kind of like the church halls – distanced from where the holy stuff went on. But Jesus was furious! He overturned the tables of the money-changers and drove them out, yelling: 'Don't turn my father's house into a marketplace!' ...

But that's just it, isn't it? ... It wasn't really the house of God: it was kind of like the neighbourhood ...

The Court of the Gentiles was the only place where a God-seeking non-Jew could go in the Temple. The Court of the Gentiles was the only place where non-Jews could experience the God of Israel. It was the *one place* where a non-Jew could go to see what Judaism was all about – and what did they see?

They saw poor people being cheated by their own. They saw empty self-serving religious practices. Every Jewish male nineteen and over had to pay an annual Temple tax of half a shekel (about two days' wages). During Passover as many as two and a quarter million Jews gathered in Jerusalem – that's a pretty big windfall. And the crunch was that the tax had to be paid in shekels: other coins were seen as unclean. The money-changers took advantage of this and charged another day's wage, on average, to change their money; and allowances were made for the money-changers to earn some interest on top – corruption was rife, and the people who could least afford it were usually the easiest victims.

And there were the animals for sacrifice. The animal had to be without blemish, and there were Temple authorities who checked to make certain the animals were acceptable. If you brought an animal from outside the Temple, it was sure to be rejected. So, although animals could be purchased for a fraction of the cost in Jerusalem, pilgrims were forced to pay well over the odds for the same thing from Temple vendors in the Court of the Gentiles.

The Court of the Gentiles – the only place where a God-seeking non-Jew could go in the Temple. The Court of the Gentiles – the only place where non-Jews could experience the God of Israel – the one place where a non-Jew could see what Judaism was all about – and what did they see?

No wonder Jesus was incensed! He overturned the tables of the money-changers and drove them out, yelling: 'Don't turn my father's house into a marketplace!'

So, tonight Jesus gets mad – angry, livid, furious, ticked off and set off – more than annoyed. Some would say he lost it! What he saw was one step too far – as far as he was concerned. But what was it that disturbed his spirit so?:

God had become a commodity, a way to make money and a way to control – the opiate of the masses.

And faith had become just rules to obey, not an enlightened path to follow.

And the Temple, built to be a house of prayer for all nations, had become a place set to serve itself. Jesus was angry at what was going on inside the Court of the Gentiles because Gentiles were included in his vision: outsiders and the vulnerable ones being ripped off were at the top of his priority list.

'A den of thieves', that's what he called the Temple.

He is speaking to the ones on the inside – the ones welcome in the inner courts and the Holy of holies:

'How dare you misrepresent the true reason for this place!' he says to them. 'We must be careful. We must be caring: because we represent God. And we cannot expect people to listen to our words and not notice our example.'

He calls them thieves, for they have stolen God from the people. And so they begin to look for a way to kill him ...

So what will we make of Jesus' outburst? Will we hear his voice and recognise it as our own? Inspired, disarmed, confused … how will we leave tonight?

Song: 'All are welcome' (from *Common Ground*)

Reflection:

If Jesus is the new Temple and we here are part of the body of Christ, then we are tents of meeting: our individual lives represent God … and so God-seekers will connect us with who God is … We must be careful. We must be caring: because we represent God. And we cannot expect people to listen to our words and not notice our example …

It has been reported that 85% of our young people between the ages of 18 and 25 leave the church, and 65% never return. We have to be brave enough to ask ourselves why. Some of their most common answers are: *'irrelevance', 'hypocrisy', 'no place for them', 'an anger and resentment to their questions'* …

When a God-seeker comes looking for a home or community, what do they find? What do they see? What do they hear? We must be careful. We must be caring: because we represent God.

Symbolic action:

Folk are invited to come and gather up the scattered coins and to drop them into a collection for a local charity (add to this collection on Easter Sunday).

After, folk pick up a card with a contemporary or biblical quote printed on it: some words of wisdom that speak about being in and of the world and God's bias for the poor, to take away and keep with them as inspiration throughout Holy Week.

Music during action: 'First-born of Mary' (by C. Richard Miles), sung by a small choir.

Closing responses:

This is the house of God:

NOT MY HOUSE OR YOUR HOUSE;
NOT BRICKS AND MORTAR, WOOD AND WALLS:
BUT A PLACE FOR EVERYONE, WITH NO BARRIERS.

This is the Word of God:

NOT JUST A RULE BOOK OR A HISTORY BOOK;
NOT SIMPLY A STORYBOOK,
BUT AN INSPIRED BEGINNING
TO A CONTINUING, UNFOLDING
LIFE TOGETHER.

We are the body of Christ:

NOT ME OR YOU OR THEM,
BUT ONE BODY WITH MANY MEMBERS –
MANY MEMBERS CALLED TO DO THEIR PART
IN ONE VERY BIG PLAN.

This place is God's.
This world is God's.
We are God's:

LET US BUILD COMMUNITY
AND GROW AND LIVE TOGETHER.
AMEN

WEDNESDAY
OF HOLY WEEK

CONVERSATIONS IN THE CROWD

First read Isaiah 50:4–9a

Person in the crowd 1:

Strange goin's on lately round here. That prophet Jesus – the one every-body's been talking about – what with all that healing and all those miracles, I don't know how he thought he'd stay out of trouble. Bound to stir folks up. Bound to make the powers-that-be a little nervous.

Person in the crowd 2:

Well, what was bound to happen *has* happened, and he's starting to lose friends and annoy High Priests. His so-called disciples have made themselves pretty scarce for best friends, and nobody seems to remember what hap-pened just a couple days ago.

Person in the crowd 1:

He was coming into the city for all the ceremonies and parties at the Passover, you know. When the people heard he was coming – they got just wild with the excitement of it. They threw their cloaks and coats on the ground. They waved palm branches in the air and shouted: 'Hosanna to the son of David. Blessed is he who comes in the name of the Lord. Hosanna in the highest!'

Person in the crowd 2:

It was just like Caesar himself was coming into town, or Pontius Pilate. Maybe that's why the Roman officials got so touchy. Somebody'd even given him a pony to ride in on.

Person in the crowd 1:

Then he made the mistake of ruffling feathers at the Temple. Heard he had a fit when he saw all the unfair goin's on there: people being cheated with Temple taxes and money-changing and touts selling sacrifices.

Typical Passover scene, but he didn't seem to know the score – he was really angry, and threw them all out, yelling and roaring like a crazy man. He seemed like a fanatic, they say … or like time was running out or something … If only he'd known then, huh?

Person in the crowd 2:

Well, they're pretty strong rumours flying about that the jig's up.

Person in the crowd 1:

His days are numbered.

Person in the crowd 2:

Things are going pear-shaped.

Person in the crowd 1:

They're bound to arrest him now, poor man. There's even this sick joke going round with the soldiers: 'He's made his cross: now he'll hang on it' … You get it, him being a carpenter and all?

Person in the crowd 2:

But surely it's up to Pilate?

Person in the crowd 1:

Pilate has been sittin' on the fence so long that his backside must be the gate and who knows which way he'll swing. He'll probably wash his hands of the whole thing and do what he always does: let somebody else decide.

Person in the crowd 2:

Well, he still has a chance then … He's healed and stood up for so many folk. The crowds have been behind him so far … And he's got those disciples who are with him everywhere he goes. After all the healing and forgiving and teaching he's done, folk will surely stand by him now.

Person in the crowd 1:

But then again, there's nothing queerer than folk …

Exit in silence.

ASKING QUESTIONS

A liturgy for the Wednesday of Holy Week

Call to worship:

Yesterday, he lost his temper, challenged the highest authority in the Temple, sent rumblings through Jerusalem. He called the High Priests thieves and the Holy of holies a 'common den' they hid in. On this Wednesday of Holy Week, they nervously approach, and ask him – just exactly who he thinks he is!

Prayer

Song: 'Before the world began' (CH4 317)

Reading: Mark 11:27–33, 12:13–17

Meditation:

Jesus:

'I will ask you one question; answer me and I will tell you by what authority I do these things.'

Narrator:

He was always doing that: answering a question with a question.

Only twelve years old, on the annual trip to Jerusalem, and he was in the Temple listening and talking to the teachers, and had lost track of time. His family had to backtrack for three days to find him! When they found him in the Temple, his mother cried out: 'Child, why have you treated us like this? Look – your father and I have been sick with worry.'

Jesus:

'Why were you searching for me? Did you not know that I'd be in my father's house?'

Narrator:

And when he was healing or teaching … When they brought the paralysed man to him, you know the one – they'd lowered him through the roof – Jesus had said to him: 'You're sins are forgiven', and the Pharisees weren't best pleased. 'Why does this fellow speak in this way? Who can forgive sins but God alone?' But Jesus saw into their hearts and said:

Jesus:

'Which is easier, to say to the paralytic: "Your sins are forgiven", or to say "Stand up, take up your mat and walk?"'

Narrator:

He was asleep in a boat, but his disciples were wide wake – a storm had blown up and they were being swamped. 'Teacher, do you not care that we are perishing?' He said to them:

Jesus:

'Why are you afraid? Have you still no faith?'

Narrator:

When they dragged the woman caught in adultery through the streets to meet him, they said: 'What should we do with her?' At first, he said nothing – actually bent down and doodled in the sand. I bet they thought they had him. But when he stood up, he said:

Jesus:

'If you are without sin, go ahead and cast the first stone' …

Narrator:

Decide for yourself: are you or aren't you? That's what he was really saying. And they dropped their stones and walked away.

When they questioned him about loving your enemies, he replied:

Jesus:

'If you love only those who love you, what reward do you have? And if you greet only your brothers and sisters, what more are you doing than others?'

Narrator:

One evening he was on a hillside teaching; the crowds had followed him from town – word had spread and there were thousands of them. It was getting late and the disciples were worried: 'Master, send them away back to the towns to get something to eat.' But he told them to feed them. 'Two hundred denarii worth of bread wouldn't feed this crowd!' But he only said:

Jesus:

'What do you have? Go and look.'

Narrator:

And they found a way.

So you see, we shouldn't be surprised that he answered the High Priests' questions with a question. He'd been doing it all his life. It was just that this time, he was asking the wrong people. The nervous, and therefore, dangerous people.

So you see, we shouldn't be surprised that sometimes there are more questions than answers: that Jesus smiles that enigmatic smile and urges us to think for ourselves.

So you see, we shouldn't be discouraged or cowed into not asking, because we come from an incredible tradition of questioners.

Song: 'God who is everywhere present on earth' (from *Songs of God's People*)

Reflective action:

We come now to a time of reflection and action. Jesus invites, welcomes and expects your questions, and he will live with you in your wrestling with them.

On the table in the centre of the church are some cards to take your questions. As the music plays, come forward and write a question to God, and then pin it to the cross by the communion table.

Know that God hears you and will help you.

Action: questions to God

And now that you've asked your questions, listen to some questions Jesus asked. And respond by singing together:

Voice 1:

'Can you see anything?'

Voice 2:

'Who touched me?'

Voice 3:

'What do you want me to do for you?'

Response: 'Listen to the word which God has spoken' (CH4 780)

Voice 1:

'Who do you say that I am?'

Voice 2:

'Why do you call me good?'

Voice 3:

'Who are you looking for?'

Response: 'Listen to the word which God has spoken'

Voice 1:

'Couldn't you stay awake?'

Voice 2:

'Why do you weep?'

Voice 3:

'My God, my God, why have you forsaken me?'

Response: 'Listen to the word which God has spoken'

Voice 1:

'Good or evil?'

Voice 2:

'Life or death?'

Voice 3:

'Don't you understand?'

Response: 'Listen to the word which God has spoken'

Voice 1:

'You will say: "Lord, when did we see you hungry?"'

Voice 2:

'Lord, when did we see you thirsty?'

Voice 3:

'When did we see you a stranger or naked or sick or in prison and did not take care of you?'

Response: 'Listen to the word which God has spoken'

Voice 1:

'Do you love me?'

Voice 2:

'Do you love me?'

Voice 3:

'Do you love me more than these?'

Response: 'Listen to the word which God has spoken'

Those are enough for tonight. Tomorrow will bring questions of its own: Will you stay or will you go? Will you deny him or stand beside him? Has he pushed things too far for you? ...

But that is for tomorrow. Tonight, leave in peace.

Song: 'Go now in peace' (by Natalie Sleeth)

MAUNDY THURSDAY

LOVE LINGERS, HOPE HOLDS ...

(Mary and the anointing of Jesus)

Opening prayer:

Come, lovers of God.
Pour out everything you have,
unstop all that you are,
all you ever dreamed in secret
that you might become ...
Do not fear it will be wasted.
For Christ is with us.
Let us worship God.

Reading: Mark 14:1–9

Song: 'Be still' (CH4 189)

Prayer:

You never skimp when it comes to us, O God of new life.
Your gifts come gushing forth without a thought for economy.
We, on the other hand, dole out our favours.

You give with no thought of getting something back.
We are thrifty folk –
and you know what they say about
one hand washing another.
You love us so much that you cannot contain yourself,
and do foolish, extravagant things to spoil your children.

We love too,
but there are limits …

We have to be careful:
we have to hold something back for a rainy day.
We don't want to be seen as foolish or as an easy touch.
You would follow us to the ends of the earth
and back again.
You will never leave us:
that is your promise.

We can only go so far:
until the road turns frightening,
the map becomes a little blurry,
the supplies are running low,
then we turn back …

Son of David, have mercy on us …
forgive us when we hide our gifts,
when we hold back what we could offer.

Forgive us when we give without grace
and expect a favour.

Forgive us when we abandon our brothers and sisters
because the road is just too long,
or the journey just too far out of our way.

God of love – you pour your forgiveness over us …
it is beautiful and sweet.
Tonight, as we remember,
let us take that beautiful sweetness with us –

and may we fling it out –
pour it over your world
with no thought for economy.
We pray all this in the name of the one
who asked us to pray together, saying:

Lord's Prayer

Song: 'Come down, O Love Divine' (CH4 489)

Reflection

Prayer:

How soon we forget.
Why do some of the most beautiful,
the most powerful and vital happenings
slip from our memories like the mist,
while we cling to hurts and imagined pains
like grim death?

God of life and love,
thank you for the lavish gifts and the beauty you shower on us:
for lovers and family and friends …
for times and places never to be forgotten …
for the raucous laughter of children
and the gentle whisper of a dear one …
We remember, and return again in thanks to you …

Tonight, as we recollect the love and betrayal in your last days,
help us to take from that high secret shelf
the sweet perfumes we have kept especially.

We will offer them without hesitation to the ones you love.
We will not count the cost – it is a gift to you.
In a world of violence, let them soothe …

We pray for folk in the news
and in places only you know of …
we pray for innocent and guilty alike.
Soothe their wounds …
Help us to do whatever we can.
In places of pain and fear – wipe their tears away …
Help us to do whatever we can.
God, who never counts what has been spent on us,
help us to be generous.
Amen

Leader:

Please join hands with your neighbour for a moment …

Feel the strength of touch, the intimacy of contact, the warmth and uniqueness of each human being ... And now, as you let go, realise that the feeling remains and the memory comforts. Listen to the truth:

Voice 1:

Love lingers, hope holds, peace perseveres long after the lover and the hoper and the peacemaker are gone.

Voice 2:

For no matter what separates you – fear, despair, anger, injustice, death itself – nothing is stronger than love. Nothing on earth or beyond can conquer it or make it cower.

Voice 1:

Love lingers, hope holds, peace perseveres long after the lover and the hoper and the peacemaker are gone.

Voice 2:

Do not miss your moment to join with the ones whose lives have proved this to be true.

When your moment comes – pour out your love with utter abandon.

Voice 1:

And you will gain everything.

Song

Closing prayer:

God, touch me:
when talking is too tiresome
and conversation has dried up
and blown away.

Hold me:
when hell has found its way to earth
and surrounds me.
Then being held may be the only way
to bring any healing there is to be had.

Embrace me:
when every effort has been made to rectify the situation,
but it is too far gone
and the end must come.

I may not respond, reach out in return,
but I will know you are there.

Blessing

WASHING HANDS AND FEET

Reading: John 13:1–16

They'd walked all day in the dirt and dust, trudged along roads and paths and hillsides. It was a dirty business. Sandals may have kept them protected from the worst of the stones, but they couldn't keep out the muck or stop the soreness creeping in. And so it was a looked-forward-to end-of-the-day ritual – foot-washing. But it was a dirty business and it was servant's work – and the more feet in the queue, the darker the water.

Jesus took a towel and took up the servant's place. He knelt in front of them, placed his hands in the ever-dirtier water and washed their feet: soothed their soreness and towelled them dry. He said: *'This is an example to you. When I'm gone – be like this.'* And it was good that he showed them what a servant was – what they were to be – because there would be other examples and they needed to know what they were called to do.

Reading: Matthew 27:15–26

He didn't want to get his hands dirty – that was servant's work. So Pilate palmed Jesus off on the crowd and denied it had anything to do with him; allowed his silence to seal Christ's fate. He took a basin of water and washed his hands of the whole sordid affair. This, too, is an example to us – and it shows that we have a choice to make. Which basin will we use, which leader will we follow, which example will make its mark on us?

What kind of person will you become: foot-washer or hand-washer? …

THE BREATH OF GOD

(for a Communion service)

Opening words:

Body of Christ, family of God, what is it that holds us together, creates the centre we share, inextricably links us to one another in a bond nothing can break? What is it? Turn to your neighbour and whisper a few words that come to mind …

Sharing

Meditation:

Friends gathered here tonight, companions who share love for each other, love for our community, love for Jesus – let me tell you a story … Think on this:

It all started/we all started when the earth was a formless void and darkness covered the face of the deep. God's Spirit breathed over the waters, and whispered 'hush' to the chaos … God breathed … in and out *(breathe in and out)* … In the very beginning …

That's one story. Here's another: The only time God ever graced us with God's name was to Moses, as he stood beside the burning bush. And God said: 'If they ask you who sent you, you can tell them this: *Yah/weh: I am* … My name,' God said, 'is *I am*: who I am, who I was, who I am yet to be … Yah/weh …'

But that's not all. Those syllables, Yah/weh, had their origin a long way back – deep in the recess of our collective memory: the sound of our breathing:

in and out ... *(Breathe in and out: 'Yah/weh ... Yah/weh'.)* God said 'I am' what holds you together; 'I am' what creates the centre you share; 'I am' what inextricably links you to one another in a bond nothing can break.

What is it, tell me now, that you and your heart whispered just a few moments ago: Was it 'Love'? ...

Tonight we gather to remember him. Tonight we gather to breathe in what he taught us, lived out in his life and died still saying:

'Love is stronger than hate.
Forgiveness is stronger than revenge.
Life is stronger than death.'

Tonight we gather round his table, and in the darkness that precedes betrayal and denial and death, we reaffirm that:

EVEN IN THE FACE OF ALL THAT,
WE CAN RISE UP AND LIVE DIFFERENT LIVES:
WHERE THE JUSTICE, PEACE AND LOVE
POURED OUT IN HIS LIFE
CAN BE RESURRECTED IN OURS.

Time of silence

Reflection:

He'd lived, breathed – shared his being with them – he'd been strong, kind, frustrated, vulnerable, tired, inspirational ... and now he faced the last supper before the last breath. What would he do, what would he say? What feeling, message, lesson, love song would he leave at the Last Supper?

Knowing that this would be the last time they were all together; knowing that this night, this meal would be ingrained in their memory; that they would relive it over and over in the years to come, what did he do?

He took a towel and a basin and began to do the servant's work. He told them to come over and to sit down and to let him wash the dirt and dust and soreness from their feet. He stooped down and untied their sandals, and washed the cares of the day away ...

He carefully patted their feet dry and looked up for the next one coming. All with good grace and gentleness. That's what he did. And there were no exceptions, no exclusions – no difference made. He washed them all – Peter who would deny him; Judas who would betray him; Thomas who would doubt him, and all who would disappear into the night. His last act was to breathe out his love before there was no breath left. Yah/weh: '*I am* for you.'

Song: 'Lord Jesus, as the shadows long are stealing' (CH4 372)

Reading: John 13:31b–35

Reflection (continued):

Knowing that this would be the last time they were all together, knowing that this night, this meal would be ingrained in their memory, that they would relive it over and over in the years to come, what did he say?

He said, '*Little children, I am with you only a little longer. You will look for me; and as I said to the Jews so I say to you: Where I am going, you cannot come. I give you a new commandment, that you love one another. Just as I have loved you, you should love one another. By this everyone will know that you are my disciple, if you have love for one another.*'

That's what he said, that's what he did – the last time they were together.

He also made them a promise: that he would never leave them orphaned and alone, but would send the Holy Spirit to keep them going in the right direction – washing feet and loving each other. And if they got sidetracked, the Spirit would swoop in, or whisper quietly but insistently, or resist their wayward path and push them back onto his.

He'd made himself clear that last time they were together, or so he'd hoped: 'Take care of each other, take the servant's role – love each other.' He went back to the very beginning at the very end.

Yah/weh – 'I am': you are connected to God through each other ... listen as the world breathes in and out. Hear God in each other's sighs ...

There will now be a moment of silence. Be attuned to your breathing. Listen to the collective Spirit of God: it connects you to every living creature ...

Time of silence

Prayers before communion:

Yah/weh ... Spirit-breath of God,
you're here ...
in the smile of our baby ...
in the laugh of our lover ...
in the song that hums away in our hearts ...
and you're here ...
in the silence of this moment ...
in the chaos that awaits us ...
in the life that spreads behind and before us ...
Hear our hearts as our spirits whisper their thank yous
round this table ...

Yah/weh ... Spirit-breath of God,
you're there ...
in the cry of their baby ...
in the heartache of a lost lover ...
in the songs their hearts are trying to sing ...
and you're there ...
in the silence of that moment ...
in the chaos that awaits them ...
in the life that spreads behind and before them ...
Hear our hearts as our spirits plead their cause
round this table.

Yah/weh ... Spirit-breath of God,
you are ...
in every cry or laugh or smile ...
And you are ...
in the silence and the chaos of the lives
that spread before and behind us ...
Whisper and plead in the ears of our hearts
till our spirits turn to you and to each other.

At the very last, Jesus reminded us of our beginning:
love breathed us into being
and we belong to each other.

Yah/weh ... Spirit-breath of God,
hold us together
here at his table.
Amen

Communion

DENIERS, DOUBTERS, BETRAYERS ALL

A Communion liturgy for Maundy Thursday

Before the service, set a box on a table in the crossing (or in another central location) with pencils and pieces of card nearby.

'The last time we spoke':

Voice 1:

Last time we spoke, I asked after the family – he said they were all fine, as far as he knew, but then he didn't see much of them now. I didn't ask him anything else. I didn't want to pry.

Voice 2:

Last time we spoke, we argued. Can't remember what about now – strange, it seemed so important at the time.

Voice 3:

Last time we spoke, he said he loved me, that he was proud of me, that there wasn't *one* thing about me that he'd change in a million years. He said that I was the best gift he and mum could ever have been given.

Voice 4:

Last time I saw her, we didn't speak. I avoided eye contact and she pretended I wasn't there. Lots of rough water under that particular bridge – still, I'd never have imagined it'd end like that.

Voice 5:

Last time we spoke, there was so much laughter that the folk at the table next to us caught it. It was contagious apparently. The stories kept coming and the wine was flowing and it was like we'd never been apart. All the years melted away and we all remembered why we'd got together in the first place. It was a wee bit of magic.

Voice 6:

Last time we spoke, we didn't know it would be the last time. So he gave me a peck on the cheek, and he tousled our youngest's hair and teased about a haircut; he waved a casual goodbye to the breakfast table and walked out the door to work. Nothing monumental said, just 'See ya later.'

Leader:

The last time we spoke ... the last time I saw him ... the last time we were together ... the last time ... What would you want to say? What would you do? What feeling, message, lesson, love song would you want to leave if you knew it was the last time? ...

Let us worship God.

Song: 'You are called to tell the story' (CH4 680)

Leader:

What would you do, what would you say? What feeling, message, lesson, love song would you want to leave if you knew it was the last time?

He gathered them in an upper room to share a meal. The friends who were there: Simon, called Peter, his brother Andrew; James and his brother John, the sons of Zebedee; Philip and Bartholomew; Thomas and Matthew the tax collector; James the son of Alphaeus, Thaddaeus; Simon the patriot, and Judas Iscariot.

And there were women who followed, helping to support them out of their own means. Maybe, I like to think, they were there too: Mary, called Magdalene; Joanna, the wife of Chuza, the manager of Herod's household; and Susanna.

Knowing that this would be the last time they were all together, knowing that this night, this meal would be ingrained in their memory and they would relive it over and over in the years to come, what did he do?

He took a towel and a basin and began to do the servant's work. He told them to come over and to sit down and to let him wash the dirt and dust and soreness from their feet. He stooped down and untied their sandals, washed the cares of the day away, leaving the remnants in a bowl at his feet. He carefully patted their feet dry and looked up for the next one coming. All with good grace and gentleness. That's what he did.

Knowing that this would be the last time they were all together, knowing that this night, this meal would be ingrained in their memory and that they would relive it over and over in the years to come, what did he say?

He said, *'Little children, I am with you only a little longer. You will look for me; and as I said to the Jews so I say to you: where I am going, you cannot come. I give you a new commandment, that you love one another. Just as I have loved you, you should love one another. By this everyone will know that you are my disciples, if you have love for one another.'*

That's what he said, that's what he did – the last time they were together. He also made them a promise: that he wouldn't leave them orphaned and alone, but would send the Holy Spirit to keep them going in the right direction – washing feet and loving each other. If they got sidetracked, the Spirit would swoop in or whisper quietly but insistently, or resist their wayward path, and push them back onto his.

He'd made himself clear about that this last time they were together, or so he'd hoped: that they were to take care of each other, take the servant's role – love each other like he'd loved them.

We come now to the table – the Last Supper. His friends were there, the twelve who were especially close to him – some of whom we may feel we know well too, because they seem to represent us: Peter who denied him, Judas who betrayed him, Thomas who doubted himself every bit as much as he doubted Jesus' return, and the others – they too represent the secret, silent ways we all fail to live by washing feet and loving each other.

With whom do you most identify tonight? Who holds your secret with them? ... Think on that as we sing a song to prepare us for communion.

Song: 'Before I take the body of my Lord' (CH4 658)

Leader:

We come to communion, the Last Supper. What do you want him to know now; what do you need to be released from, upheld in, given strength for?

There are four stations. Four folk stand in front of them *(e.g. Eucharistic ministers, elders, leaders)*:

Peter who denied him ...

Judas who betrayed him ...

Thomas who doubted himself every bit as much as he doubted Jesus' return ...

The others who represent all the secret, silent ways we fail to live by washing feet and loving each other ...

With whom do you most identify tonight? Who holds your secret with them? Go to them for communion, knowing that Christ loved them to the end and loves you too.

Hear the story of that last time together ...

Bible reading: 1 Corinthians 11 ('On the night that Jesus was betrayed ...')

Leader:

Come – deniers, doubters, betrayers all.
This is for you.

Come – saints and sinners and prodigal children.
This is for you.

Come, the table is laid, the food is set out and the wine is poured.
All for you ...

Communion *(soft music played underneath)*

Communion prayers *(said as folk receive the elements; prayer said by the leader to each person):*

Peter:

(With the bread) You are forgiven the times
you've denied who you are.

(With the wine) You are forgiven the times
you've denied who He is and what others need.

Judas:

(With the bread) You are forgiven the times
you've betrayed yourself and others.

(With the wine) You are forgiven the times
you've betrayed Him.

Thomas:

(With the bread) You are forgiven the times
you've doubted yourself and others.

(With the wine) You are forgiven the times
you've doubted Him.

The others:

(With the bread) You are forgiven
all the secret, silent ways you've failed.

(With the wine) You are forgiven
the times you've not washed feet and loved others.

'The last time we spoke' (conclusion):

Voice 1:

Last time we spoke, I asked after the family – he said they were all fine, as far as he knew, but then he didn't see much of them now. We went for a walk because it seemed he needed someone to listen. I didn't ask him anything else. I just let him talk.

Voice 2:

Last time we spoke, we argued. When I got home I realised I couldn't remember what it was even about – strange, it had seemed so important at the time; so I called and we set things right.

Voice 3:

Last time we spoke, he said he loved me, that he was proud of me, that there wasn't *one* thing about me that he'd change in a million years. He said that I was the best gift he and mum could ever have been given.

Voice 4:

Last time I saw her, we almost didn't speak. I was avoiding eye contact and she was pretending I wasn't there. Lots of rough water under that particular bridge – still, I'd never have imagined it'd end like that. So I took a deep breath, walked over and said, 'Can we talk?'

Voice 5:

Last time we spoke, there was so much laughter that the folk at the table next to us caught it. It was contagious apparently. The stories kept coming and the wine was flowing and it was like we'd never been apart. All the years melted away and we all remembered why we'd got together in the first place. It was a wee bit of magic.

Voice 6:

Last time we spoke, we didn't know it would be the last time. So he gave me a peck on the cheek, and he tousled our youngest's hair and teased about a haircut; he waved a casual goodbye to the breakfast table and walked out the door to work. Nothing monumental said, just 'See ya later.'

Leader:

What would you do, what would you say? What feeling, message, lesson, love song would you want to leave if you knew it was the last time? ...

Music will play quietly now for 10 minutes or so to give you time to reflect. There is a box on the table in the crossing and pencils and pieces of card. If you have something to say, to God or to someone else, take a moment and write it down and place it in the box. No one will read it. It is between you and God.

Action: *(writing a message)*

Song: 'Brother, sister, let me serve you' (CH4 694)

Benediction:

This is the last time they were together before he gave his all, emptied himself; before the powers-that-be decided that his goodness was really just too much of a threat. The ultimate fate of his message and mission would be in the hands of the likes of us – deniers, doubters, betrayers all – saints and sinners and prodigal children. Tonight, promise him that you'll do your best, that you'll try your hardest, that you'll let his Holy Spirit work in you ...

Beloved of God,
go out in peace.
God loves you, Jesus too –
the Spirit waits to walk home with you this night
and for evermore.
Amen

The Leader takes a big candle and goes out ahead of folk.

THE DAYS HAVE GROWN DARKER

We are all Peter

1st reading: Luke 22:54–62

The days have grown darker … The palm branches have dried up, the perfume has been poured out, the hosannas have faded away, the crowds have gone home, but they will return in a different mood …

They have taken our Jesus away …

He went without a struggle – he said hardly a word.

He set his face like flint, and will not turn back. The fate of the Lamb of God has been sealed …

And there has already been so much heartache: the agony in the garden, the sting of the kiss, and now, the cut of betrayal, worse than any sword.

Peter was following, at a distance, not the right-hand man now, but checking out the lay of the land …

'I don't know him … I'm not one of them … I don't even know what you're talking about.'

How easily the lies slipped out. How quickly he evaluated the lay of the land.

How long before it registered with him … how long before he realised what he'd done? Did the cock-crow send off alarm bells? … Did his eyes lock with Jesus – the betrayed one?

Or did it take time? … Did it sink in slowly as he wept?

When the days grow darker … When the palm branches have dried up, the perfume has been poured out, the hosannas have faded away; when you find that the friendly crowds have all gone home, only to be replaced by one in a different mood, what will you say?

'I don't know him … I'm not one of them … I don't even know what you're talking about.'

We are all Peter: his story is ours … and we know when we've denied him; it registers sometimes with alarm bells: when we hear ourselves give in to what we think folk want to hear, rather than what we know to be true … or when our eyes lock with someone we've hurt, let down or even betrayed, and sometimes it sinks in slowly … takes time to creep into our conscience …

Today, let us confess our denial of him when he needs us most …

Time of silence …

But let us leave comforted, because we are forgiven and loved, and still called to be the rocks on which he builds his church.

We are all Judas

2nd reading: John 13:21–30

Judas is the traitor … He's identified, pointed out, caught red-handed, guilty as sin can be.

How easy it is to blame. How convenient to have someone to point at to say: 'There you go: you're the problem, not me.' What a relief to know that you're in the clear …

But wait. If we look more closely, this story speaks to us in a different way about this deep, dark business of betrayal.

For no one in that room was sure. No one felt safe. No one was certain that he was not the one Jesus was talking about.

All of them were haunted by thoughts, by doubts ... What one of them hadn't at one time thought about giving up on him? ... What one of them hadn't been secretly disappointed by his refusal to condemn the ones who weren't in the group, or embarrassed by his radical ways and claims? Who hadn't, at some time, in some way, betrayed him? ...

On this night, as the day grows darker ... let's listen with our eyes wide open and know that betrayal belongs to us all. We are all Judas: his story is ours.

If we are ultimately to stand with Jesus, we must confront our betraying thoughts and learn from them ... We must admit to the thoughts we all have that give up on him somehow ... We must own up to the times when we have been secretly disappointed by his refusal to condemn the ones who aren't in the group, when we've been embarrassed by his radical ways or claims ... When we wished he wasn't so quick to forgive and forget.

Time of silence ...

The days have grown darker ... The palm branches have dried up, the perfume has been poured out, the hosannas have faded away, the crowds have gone home, but they will return in a different mood ...

They have taken our Jesus away ...

He went without a struggle – he said hardly a word.

He set his face like flint, and will not turn back. The fate of the Lamb of God has been sealed ...

And there is more heartache to come ...

And I can't help but wonder what might have happened:

If Judas had remained in the upper room and had refused his thirty pieces of silver ...

If the crowds had resolutely refused to turn ...

If the disciples had stayed awake in the garden and stood their ground.

If Pilate had taken matters into his own hands instead of washing them ...

If someone, somewhere, had stayed with Jesus ...

Tonight we remember how the King of heaven was on earth betrayed, rejected and sent to his death by religious people who thought they were doing the right thing; by a friend who thought he knew more than God; by other friends who were too frightened to know what to do; by crowds who changed their hearts and minds as often as they changed their sandals; and by one man who had the power to change it all, but no courage to do anything.

And we have come knowing that we would have done exactly the same ... But we believe, and in the life of Christ we see, that the love of God is greater than the sin of the world.

When the tide turned and the fate of the Lamb of God had been sealed, he let them do their worst, until their worst was done. And when it was finished, it would have been all over had he not cried: *'Father, forgive them'* ... and started the revolution ...

STAY WITH ME

When discretion is the better
or at least the safer
part of valour –
when might is insisting it's right
and we are caught or swayed or afraid of its power;
when news and neighbours tell us that there *is* fire
behind all that smoke,
and that we'd better jump on the bandwagon
before it leaves us behind,
and we are sorely tempted,
tempted to forget the words you spoke in the stillness –
be with us God.

Give us the courage to stay with you,
when words like honesty, justice, mercy, compassion
are renamed weakness.
Help us to stay with our brother Jesus ...

Sung response: 'O brother Jesus, where have we left you? (from *Love from Below*)

When our ideals are in danger of being betrayed
in the everyday decisions that we have to make –
decisions that ask us to choose whether we save money today
or consider the planet for tomorrow;
whether we enjoy a bit more of what keeps us comfortable,
or offer support to somebody we've never met
and aren't likely to;

whether we opt into the very sensible adages:
'Look out for number one'
and 'Birds of a feather flock together',
or take our chances with the stories Jesus told
about the Good Samaritan
and the pearl of great price –
be with us God.

Give us the courage to stay with you,
when we have to decide
in the real world
whether honesty, justice, mercy, compassion
are worth sacrificing.
Help us to stay with our brother Jesus ...

Sung response: 'O brother Jesus, where have we left you?'

For the times when we've left you behind
or shied away from you,
or been embarrassed by the extremes to which you go
to make your point,
forgive us.
When we lag behind or hide away,
or run as far and as fast as we can
away from your embrace,
forgive us.
And not only forgive,
but wait ...
and walk with us again.

God our maker,
you never leave us.
You only love us.
Help us to stay with our brother Jesus …

Sung response: 'O brother Jesus, where have we left you?'

TWIST AND TURN

Reading: John 13:21–30

There is a final perplexing twist in this story: one to wrestle with as we walk with him into Good Friday …

The disciple whom Jesus loved – the confidant who knew that Judas would betray his friend – did nothing.

Could he not understand what was happening?

Could he simply not fathom such betrayal?

Did he not know what to do: and so did nothing?

Did he hope against hope that Jesus would do something himself, or that one of the others would act?

Why doesn't the disciple whom Jesus loved do anything about this betrayal?

Why doesn't he go after Judas, follow him, talk him round, hammer him one – stop him?!

Why? … Who knows.

There is a final perplexing truth in our story – one to wrestle with as we walk with him into Good Friday …

Why don't we, when we know something is wrong, act to stop it?

Why don't we follow up on policies that are unjust, or speak up when we see others oppressed or hurt? …

Do we hope against hope that somebody else will see to what we've seen, but have turned away from?

The final perplexing twist in this story: one to wrestle with as we walk with him into Good Friday ...

Prayer

When the voice of Jesus whispers in our hearts,
when we see the hopes of Jesus
betrayed in this world,
may we not twist
and turn away.

GOOD FRIDAY

GETTING OUR HANDS DIRTY

A liturgy for Good Friday

Preparation:

Before the service, light a central candle and darken-down the church. Fill the font, or a large container, with earth (compost and leaves). Sprinkle it with water so that during the action earth will stick to people's hands ...

Split up the Bible readings and prayers between the Leader, Voice 1, Voice 2, etc.

Introduction:

Conversationally

Voice 1:

The only reason this is Good Friday is because we are here telling his story – still.

Voice 2:

The only thing good about this story is that he kept on with the loving even in the face of unspeakable cruelty and injustice – still.

Voice 1:

There is nothing good about cruelty and injustice. Nothing that makes it worthwhile, nothing that makes it OK, nothing that takes away the slicing edgy hardness, yet it goes on – still.

Voice 2:

On this Friday, when the goodness of God was put to an unfair, biased test, and won, we struggle on – still. Will we stay with him, or will we go? Will we deny we ever knew him, or will we face the time of testing beside him? And when it is our turn to forgive each other, will we be able to say 'Father, forgive them', when we know what they've done?

Song: 'Great God, your love has called us here' (CH4 484, omit verse 4)

Leader:

Why this execution? Why this man? Why do we gather in the dark and silence to mark his death when, sadly, it is not unique, and never has been. In his day, the crucified lined the streets, a macabre reminder that power hates challenge of any kind. The story is eerie in its utter transference to situations today and throughout history – the push by the desperate powerful against the pedestal of high ideals. No matter how genuine and firm the ideals, they look for a tiny point of vulnerability from which to begin their teetering and toppling.

The predictable unpredictability of the crowds, who at one moment shout their support, yet at the first sign of smoke, assume fire and, just as quickly, withdraw and doubt and even bay for blood – who realise too late that they've been duped, and then stand sadly on the sidelines wringing their hands, wishing things had been different. Then they go home and live exactly the same way – until the next time.

And there are the ones more closely involved – the friends and colleagues and hangers-on who abandon ship and deny knowledge and even betray.

There are the ones in a position to stop the injustice, who choose to turn away and wash their hands of the whole sad, sordid affair.

The characters take up their positions and the play begins, again and again and again.

Crucifixions happen all the time. The story is harrowing because it is so familiar.

So why this execution? Why this man? Why do we gather in the dark and silence to mark his death when, sadly, it is not unique, and never has been?

Perhaps that is exactly why. Because it represents the inhumanity we are capable of – even towards the totally innocent and completely pure: the very embodiment of goodness. Perhaps his words: *'What you do to the least of these, you do to me'* echo tonight especially. Perhaps his words from last night still sit in your mind and heart: *'This is my body broken for you.'* And perhaps the words he has yet to say are our only hope: *'Father, forgive them, for they know not what they do.'* We didn't know then – we know now – and we must change. Change is the hope, and forgiveness opens the door.

So tonight, we gather and remember his death. We mourn his loss and we grieve the part we play in it. And we consider the crucifixions we witness today, for they are the real reason for our corporate grief.

There will now be some music and time for reflection. Afterwards we will hear part of the story and respond to it in prayer together. Allow yourself space to grieve and grow ...

Music/time for reflection

Bible readings/prayer/sung response:

(Bible readings: Luke 22:39–46; Luke 22:47–53; Luke 22:54–62; Luke 22:63–65, 23:13–25; Luke 23:33–38, 23:44–46, NRSV)

He came out and went, as was his custom, to the Mount of Olives; and the disciples followed him. When he reached the place, he said to them, 'Pray that you may not come into the time of trial.' Then he withdrew from them about a stone's throw, knelt down, and prayed, 'Father, if you are willing, remove this cup from me; yet, not my will but yours be done.' Then an angel from heaven appeared to him and gave him strength. In his anguish he prayed more earnestly, and his sweat became like great drops of blood falling down on the ground. When he got up from prayer, he came to the disciples and found them sleeping because of grief, and he said to them, 'Why are you sleeping? Get up and pray that you may not come into the time of trial.'

Prayer:

Good God, what have we done? When we've been blind to your pain, when we've been asleep on the job you left us to get on with, when we are not willing to drink from your cup, forgive us. We do not understand the extent of what we do.

Sung response: 'O brother Jesus, where have we left you?' (from *There Is One Among Us*)

Bible reading:

While he was still speaking, suddenly a crowd came, and the one called Judas, one of the twelve, was leading them. He approached Jesus to kiss him; but Jesus said to him, 'Judas, is it with a kiss that you are betraying the

Son of Man?' When those who were around him saw what was coming, they asked, 'Lord, should we strike with the sword?' Then one of them struck the slave of the High Priest and cut off his right ear. But Jesus said, 'No more of this!' And he touched his ear and healed him. Then Jesus said to the chief priests, the officers of the Temple police, and the elders who had come for him, 'Have you come out with swords and clubs as if I were a bandit? When I was with you day after day in the Temple, you did not lay hands on me. But this is your hour, and the power of darkness!'

Prayer:

Good God, what have we done? When we betray you with our hearts and with our lips, when we choose to respond with violence instead of understanding, when we carefully claim to be with you only when and where it is safe, and then decry you when things get hard, forgive us. We do not understand the extent of what we do.

Sung response: 'O brother Jesus, where have we left you?'

Bible reading:

Then they seized him and led him away, bringing him into the High Priest's house. But Peter was following at a distance. When they had kindled a fire in the middle of the courtyard and sat down together, Peter sat among them. Then a servant-girl, seeing him in the firelight, stared at him and said, 'This man also was with him.' But he denied it, saying, 'Woman, I do not know him.' A little later someone else, on seeing him, said, 'You also are one of them.' But Peter said, 'Man, I am not!' Then about an hour later still another kept insisting, 'Surely this man also was with him; for he is a Galilean.' But Peter said, 'Man, I do not know what you are talking about!' At that moment, while he was still speaking, the cock crowed. The Lord turned and looked at Peter. Then Peter remembered the word of the Lord, how he had said to him, 'Before the cock crows today, you will deny me three times.' And he went out and wept bitterly.

Prayer:

Good God, what have we done? Walked away sometimes. Ran away sometimes. We have remained silent when we should have spoken, and we have shouted the loudest when there were other voices to protect our anonymity. When you became a liability, we denied we ever knew you. Have mercy. We do not understand the extent of what we do.

Sung response: 'O brother Jesus, where have we left you?'

Bible reading:

Now the men who were holding Jesus began to mock him and beat him; they also blindfolded him and kept asking him, 'Prophesy! Who is it that struck you?' They kept heaping many other insults on him ...

Pilate then called together the chief priests, the leaders, and the people, and said to them, 'You brought me this man as one who was perverting the people; and here I have examined him in your presence and have not found this man guilty of any of your charges against him. Neither has Herod, for he sent him back to us. Indeed, he has done nothing to deserve death. I will therefore have him flogged and release him.'

Then they all shouted out together, 'Away with this fellow! Release Barabbas for us!' (This was a man who had been put in prison for an insurrection that had taken place in the city, and for murder.) Pilate, wanting to release Jesus, addressed them again; but they kept shouting, 'Crucify,

crucify him!' A third time he said to them, 'Why, what evil has he done? I have found in him no ground for the sentence of death; I will therefore have him flogged and then release him.' But they kept urgently demanding with loud shouts that he should be crucified; and their voices prevailed. So Pilate gave his verdict that their demand should be granted. He released the man they asked for, the one who had been put in prison for insurrection and murder, and he handed Jesus over as they wished.

Prayer:

Good God, what have we done? Cruelty and callousness, anger and oppression, use and abuse of power – when we are guilty as sin of being unkind, when we take advantage of our advantages, forgive us. When we wash our hands even though keeping them in the mire might build a new and better outcome, forestall us. Christ, have mercy. We do not understand the extent of what we do.

Sung response: 'O brother Jesus, where have we left you?'

Bible reading:

When they came to the place that is called the Skull, they crucified Jesus. Then Jesus said, 'Father, forgive them; for they do not know what they are doing.' And they cast lots to divide his clothing. And the people stood by, watching; but the leaders scoffed at him, saying, 'He saved others; let him save himself if he is the Messiah of God, his chosen one!' The soldiers also mocked him, coming up and offering him sour wine, and saying, 'If you are the King of the Jews, save yourself!' There was also an inscription over him, 'This is the King of the Jews.'

It was now about noon, and darkness came over the whole land until three in the afternoon, while the sun's light failed; and the curtain of the Temple was torn in two. Then Jesus, crying with a loud voice, said, 'Father, into your hands I commend my spirit.' Having said this, he breathed his last.

Prayer:

Good God, what have we done? We have watched at a distance and wrung our hands in ineffective sympathy, we've been far too ready to mock and judge, and we are so easily swayed. Christ, have mercy. We do not understand the extent of what we do.

Song: 'The servant' (from *Enemy of Apathy*)

Introduction to symbolic action:

Leader:

The Lenten journey ends here. Now all we can do is wait to see if hope lives again. On Ash Wednesday, traditionally these words are said, as the ashes are placed on people's foreheads: *'From dust you have come, from dust you shall return.'*

On this night, as we remember the betrayal, the denial, the abandonment and the washing of the hands, remember that until you die, you are not to wash your hands of the world's troubles, or abandon your brother in his fear or your sister in her oppression. Do not turn your face away in denial when children cry. And when power seeks to crush innocence and goodness, reach out your hand and do not hold back.

In the font tonight there is no water for washing, but earth. Jesus got his hands dirty and we need to do the same. At the end of the service, please follow me to the font and place your hands in the dirt. Pray and promise that the next time crucifixion looms, you will act differently.

There is no benediction tonight. That, hopefully, will come later. We will leave in silence.

The worship leader then covers the communion table with a black cloth.

Jesus said: 'I am the Light of the world.'

The leader then blows or snuffs out the central candle.

Action: *(getting our hands dirty)*

Sally Foster-Fulton, with Ruth Burgess

HANDS-ON

'Whatever your hand finds to do, do with your might ...'
Ecclesiastes 9:10

God, I bet you have dirty hands –
caked with soil from creation, dusty from the road,
from times when you've helped friends up when
they've fallen;
and creased and cracked
from your endless dipping into the waters of chaos
(desperately wishing to bail us out).

I bet they're weather-worn and work-sore hands,
definitely at the end of rolled-up sleeves ...

And how we imagine your hands is important,
because your hands mirror your heart.

God of the dirty hands,
you didn't call us to be apart from the world –
but in it up to our elbows.
You didn't ask us to fold our hands
and pray piously in a quiet corner,
but to offer them outright
in the corners of the world where
people have been pushed and driven
and can't get out.
You never asked us to be indifferent,
but to try to *make* a difference.

So, God of the dirty hands,
do not let us deceive ourselves.
When we choose to
wash our hands of the whole sad affair,
we aren't remaining neutral:
we're siding with the powerful.

When we choose to wash our hands,
we are playing right into the hands of those
who depend on apathy
to stay on top.

Take our hands, God,
and put them to work:
our hearts will follow.
Amen

LIFTED HIGH ON YOUR CROSS

Opening responses:

Jesus Christ, lover of all, you raise us up –
our spirits, our expectations, our hopes.
JESUS CHRIST, LOVER OF ALL, YOU RAISE US UP.

Jesus Christ, lover of all, you hold us close:
when all seems lost, when hard times come,
when we don't know where else to turn.
JESUS CHRIST, LOVER OF ALL, YOU HOLD US CLOSE.

Jesus Christ, lover of all, you lead us forward –
beyond our dreams,
to places we didn't expect, or even want to go:
to a new life and way.
JESUS CHRIST, LOVER OF ALL, YOU LEAD US FORWARD.

And we will follow.
Jesus Christ, lover of all, help us to follow you.

Song: 'Lifted high on your cross' (CH4 386)

Reflection:

'Lifted high on your cross …'

Why do we lift this up? Surely we could have come up with another symbol
to front our faith. The stone rolled away – Christ ascending to God: that's a
beautiful image. The baby in the manger, the king on the donkey … why

the cross? Why would we want this image always in front of us? Why do we have this image as a representation of what we believe, of what ultimately saves us?

We are Christians – followers of the Christ who died on this cross because he loved us, because he had something to teach the world, and would not be deterred – even by death.

Look at the cross ... and remember him when your heart wants to betray someone you love ...

Look at the cross ... and remember him when you are tempted to deny who you are or what you believe ...

Look at the cross ... and remember him when you want to wash your hands of the whole awful mess you see in the world ...

The cross cries out its warning: against loving yourself more than others; against fearing Truth that may cost you something; against selling what is priceless for thirty pieces of silver ...

Do not ever forget this symbol – do not ever let it become just a piece of jewellery, or a work of art, or a design for a stained-glass window. It should burn in your heart and mind and spirit every day.

Why do we lift this up? Surely we could have come up with another symbol to front our faith. The stone rolled away – Christ ascending to God: that's a beautiful image. The baby in the manger, the king on the donkey ... why the cross? Why would we want this image always in front of us? Why do we have this image as a representation of what we believe, of what ultimately saves us? Maybe because the cross has the power to change the world.

We are Christians – followers of the Christ who died on this cross because he loved us. And we are Christians because we believe he had something to give the world, and that he was not defeated – even by death.

He calls us to *resurrection* – not resuscitation of our old life, but resurrection to an entirely new way. We are called into death with him – death to all that holds us down or keeps us apart, death to our meaningless clinging to that which will crumble and fall.

We are called to new life through Jesus Christ, who died forgiving and lives on with that message still singing – because you sing:

'Lifted high on your cross,
drawing all folk,
drawing all folk;
lifted high on your cross,
drawing all folk to you.'

Lift him high. Never put that symbol down. Let it live in you.

Let it sing out its truth that, even when we fail, God remains, love prevails and we are forgiven and freed. Resurrection happens today. Amen

CRUCIFIXION

Reading: John 19:16–30

Crucifixion – we shouldn't be too surprised –
we shouldn't really be altogether shocked either.
I mean it's what we do, you know,
to the pure at heart,
to the folk naive enough to think that
their one lone brave act
can change a system,
bring down an unjust empire,
make a difference
in the course of history.

They are crucified.
Not just stopped or silenced or shut down –
but crushed, humiliated, made an example of:
power does not like to be challenged.

If we're brave enough to face it,
we admit
it still happens today.

It happens in small ways in the playground
when bullies find a target;
it happens again in high school,
and later in the boardroom
as people shove and jostle for a place
(that scramble to the top of the heap inevitably leaves
boot-prints on some).

We see it on a larger scale in the news
as oppressed folk stand up against regimes:
think Tiananmen Square, Libya, Egypt, Syria ...
The story is eerie in its utter transference
to situations today and throughout history –
the push by the desperate powerful
against the pedestal of high ideals.

Crucifixions happen all the time.

The story is harrowing
because it is so familiar.

Reflection: Who is being crucified today? ...

HOLY SATURDAY

'PREPARE TO FOLLOW ME'

Worship for Holy Saturday

This service takes place in a graveyard.

Call to worship:

There will come a time
when everything around you will be gone –
blown away like dust ...
But there will never come a time
when the wind-breath of God ceases to blow,
when the Spirit sleeps.
Let us worship what holds everything fast.

Solo voice: 'From the falter of breath' (CH4 730)

Reflection:

In a graveyard I used to visit, there is an ancient headstone which sits broken in two pieces against a back wall near a river path. Its words are faded, but still call to passers-by.

I wonder how many people have noticed it there. I wonder if they realise what it says:

'Remember, man, as you go by,
as you are now so once was I.
As I am now, so you shall be.
Prepare, therefore, to follow me.'

Folk walk past that gravestone every day, but I wonder how often they stop, and reflect on the reality that there will come a time when they won't be here: when they will join all these: when we will all go back to the earth of which we are a part …

Today is not simply the day before we celebrate the empty tomb; today is the day set aside to hallow the emptiness: to enter into the space where things feel off-kilter, where we embrace the unknown-ness of death and grief.

Life and death and eternity are mysteries, and today acknowledges that. Holy Saturday is not about answering these questions, which will grow deeper, not easier. Today, we are called to mourn and wonder and think about our own fragile impermanence. It's hard to fathom – this mortality of ours.

Solo voice: 'From the falter of breath'

Reflection:

I remember going to a neighbour's funeral once: we were friendly with the family. Tony's grandchildren played with us – and his wife always fed you ridiculously good food in vast amounts whenever you dropped by.

At the end of the funeral, before the casket was carried out of the church, the priest walked over, and laid his hand upon it and said to the family: 'It is written "He is not here". Neither then is Tony.'

He is not here, so where is he? Tradition tells us that Jesus spent the hours between the Crucifixion and the Resurrection 'harrowing the halls of Hell' – Jesus' rap on the door sending a shiver down the spine of all who hear it. Is that where he is? In death as in life, freeing the captives, bringing his people safely home? I like that tradition.

Life and death and eternity are mysteries: today is not about answering these questions which will grow deeper, not easier. Today, we are called to mourn and wonder and think about our own fragile impermanence. It's hard to fathom – this mortality of ours.

'It is written: "He is not here". Neither then is Tony,' the priest said. So, where is he? I still see Tony in the gentle face of his granddaughter. His family live on in ways that do him honour.

Where is he? Truth is, none of us knows – but he's not here.

Solo voice: 'From the falter of breath'

Time for reflection:

Think of someone you love who has died. Paint a picture in your mind – with words, with memories, with lessons … And remember that person here in the silence.

Time of quiet …

'Remember, man, as you go by,
as you are now so once was I.
As I am now, so you shall be.
Prepare, therefore, to follow me.'

Today, we allow ourselves to think about death.

Before you go, take a flower and visit one of the graves. Read the gravestone. Think of the person and the impact made by the life of one human being – imagine the love and laughter, the heartache and bittersweet beauty contained in their time.

Say a prayer for the person and for their family and friends.

Pray that what will live on in the people you touch will reflect the gift of life you have been given.

Tomorrow will come soon enough. Amen

... a prayer for the person and for their family and friends.

May that when they will live on in the people you touch will reflect the gift of life you have been given.

Tomorrow will come soon enough. Amen.

EASTER SUNDAY

THE ROCK

You know, I was no ordinary rock. I mean, I don't really come off right in those stories.

No, it wasn't like I was just shoved in front of a hole.

I was special: sculpted and crafted every bit as carefully as that cross they hung him on.

They'd smoothed my hard, weathered edges so I'd roll. Then they'd struggled under my weight, dug trenches for me to follow up the hill a little ways, and nailed pegs in the ground so I'd stay put until it was time.

And I was huge: a giant turned into a tool designed to keep things out and in.

They'd carried his broken body into the tomb as the sun set on Friday night and placed it, lifeless, on one of my brother stones. Then it was my turn. After they'd removed the pegs, and I'd found *my* final resting place, nobody was gonna turf me out of the way. I knew my job. I closed things up, put a final end to things. I was the seal ... rock solid ... immovable. That was me.

Well, that's what you'd think, wouldn't you? That's what anyone would expect. But then, we'd had dealings with him before:

In the beginning, we'd been putty in his hands: the stuff of creation, and we'd given way then.

When the Israelites were thirsty in the desert, the order had been given to strike us and we'd give water. We obeyed.

Into stones as solid as me had been chiselled truths so eternal that they would echo down time long after the original stones had turned to dust and blown away.

We'd even had personal encounters with the one I wouldn't be able to hold:

He'd been tempted to turn us into bread, but he'd known that life was more than just existing.

And later on, he'd challenged men to be the first to cast us if they were innocent, and they threw us away.

Only a few days ago, the powerful who silenced him were told we would shout aloud if his followers were stopped.

I knew my job. I closed things up, put a final end to things. I was the seal: rock solid, immovable; that was me. Well, that's what you'd think, wouldn't you?

But there is something far more powerful than me: something that can never be closed up or ended; one thing that is truly immovable. In this Jesus Christ, I met my match and my Maker. He moved me, and he'll move you too.

EASTER PRAYERS

Easter has come

Easter has come.
And so it begins, God.

Send your Spirit into our locked places,
into our hidden rooms,
into the corners where fear and betrayal,
where self-doubt and doubt in you
keep us cowering.
Send your Spirit there,
for it begins there.

Call us down into the world you love
and put us to work.
Call us down into the streets you walk
and have our footsteps keep to yours.
Call us down into the places where you are needed
and make us your body.

Easter has come,
and so it begins, God.

When we would rather you stay in the pigeonholes
we've crammed you in,
when we would rather you conform
to the social and cultural norms
we have decided are appropriate,
when we would rather you keep

your opinions to yourself,
forgive us and do your will anyway.

Easter has come
and so it begins, God.

It begins –
again and again and again.
Amen

God, building-uncontained

God, building-uncontained,
too often we call to you from a small, hidden
upper room in your house.
So far off and distant at times are we,
so separated by time and space and everyday living –
by fear and desire and confused apathy –
that we seem destined to live in a cramped space
of our own design.
Too often, we treat your world
like a boarding house
instead of home.

As we gather here today,
call us out of our corners
and into your family.
Open the doors of our hearts and
the windows of our minds –
give us a room with a view,
that we might see.

God, building-uncontained,
you are rebuilding –
breaking down the walls that divide
and designing an open-plan community with your
creative, evolving Spirit.
Today, call us to work with you –
to tear down walls,
to open dark places too long closed,
to help you create a place for all your children.

Help us to step up into the places you need us,
and out of those narrow boxes
we've built in a vain attempt to try to keep it together
alone.

Come, you who house and hold us:
join our hearts and spirits and minds,
for you dwell in each of us.

God, building-uncontained –
come, and with your peace
contain us all in all.
Amen

Spirit-wind

Spirit-wind, blowing life into our beings …
Spirit-wind, moving over our troubled waters …
Spirit-wind, opening locked doors and secret corners …

We find you in the most unexpected places –
in the smile of a lover,

in the laugh of a child.
We see your Spirit shining
from the eyes of a perfect stranger.
Lord Jesus Christ,
thank you for finding us.

Spirit-wind, blowing life into our beings ...
Spirit-wind, moving over our troubled waters ...
Spirit-wind, opening locked doors and secret corners ...

We find you in the most unexpected places –
in the sadness of the desolate,
in the cry of a child.
We see your Spirit staring out
from the eyes of perfect strangers.

Lord Jesus Christ,
thank you for finding us.

We pray for the desolate who find themselves
in places unimaginable:
where there is grief, help us bring comfort,
where there is pain, help us bring relief,
where there is anger and violence
and what appears to be no way out,
help us discover new ways to meet in the middle
and begin the clear-up.

Lord Jesus Christ,
we find you,
and when we can't
you find us ...

Be with us now
as we bring the ones we know and love to you
who also love them ...

Stir us and send us out

Spirit God,
comforter and challenger –
you stir us and send us out.

Away from the towers and cities we build to keep
our little lives safe,
down from upper rooms where we hide
too afraid to hope –
out into the wide world
where we are called to live as Jesus did:
loving in the face of everything.

Spirit of God,
when we shelter in corners to avoid the persistent push
of your compelling Spirit,
forgive us.

When we forge ahead,
tilted against your wind and will,
forgive us.

And don't just forgive,
but keep blowing
until we turn.

SIGNS OF NEW LIFE

Plan for an Easter Sunday walk and treasure hunt

This can be a stand-alone activity or be part of an Easter sunrise service (if there is a trek involved). Some items need to be placed beforehand, and each child or family group needs an explanation sheet. Here's what folk are looking for, etc:

1. Hunting for Easter eggs (use plastic or real eggs – and roll them together):

   'Baby birds and other animals come from eggs – so eggs are signs of new life.'

2. Bulbs (make these easy-to-grow bulbs), or use seed-pots:

   'When you plant seeds and bulbs, you help make new plants. Take these bulbs home and take care of them. You can plant them today and they will bloom in July or August *(depending on area)*. Plant them about 4 inches deep, water them – and watch for signs of new life.'

3. Baby animals (use small stuffed animals or have volunteers crochet bunnies, chicks …):

   'Baby animals, just like baby people, need love and care if they are to grow up. If you find a 'baby animal' on our walk, pick it up and promise that you will look after creatures who are smaller than you, and will care for all of God's creation.'

4. Butterflies (there are a lot of templates out there: its best to use ones that won't fall apart if they get soggy. If you leave them uncoloured, the children can decorate them themselves: bring markers, crayons …):

'A butterfly begins life as a caterpillar. Butterflies show us that we are all meant to become something new! There is a special plan for each one of us. Find a butterfly to decorate.'

5. Jesus taught us to be fair:

'At some point along the walk, you will come across a "starting line". When you find it, gather all together and wait for the signal to start. This is a race with a difference, because the goal is to cross the line together! Good luck! Winners can all choose a prize at the end that reminds them to be fair.'

(You need to set this up beforehand and have an adult in charge of the starting and prizes: fairtrade chocolate or bananas ...)

6. Jesus taught us to be kind:

'Hunt for friendship bracelets. Give one to a friend, or to someone you don't know that well yet, for Easter.'

(Bracelets can be bought from a One World shop or volunteers can make them.)

7. Jesus taught us to forgive each other:

'Jesus taught us to say "I'm sorry". When we apologise, admit when we're wrong, and forgive each other, we offer new life to relationships.'

There are two things to look for:

A. 'Get Out of Trouble Free' card – not to keep, but to give.

This card entitles the recipient
to get out of trouble free.
You are forgiven – no strings attached!

B. 'I'm Sorry' card

This card entitles the receiver to choose one gift:

– a cuddle

– one chore done by the giver.

(The cards can be made like coupons or vouchers – use your imagination!)

NOT BECAUSE YOU'RE GONE

(A reflection for an Easter sunrise service)

A few years ago, I scattered the ashes of my friend Bob on the top of Dumyat in the Ochil Hills, near Stirling. It was one of his last requests.

So one sunny Saturday, his wife and child, his son-in-law and grand-daughter, and about thirty friends, made the trek up with Bob's ashes in a rucksack. Nestled alongside them was his last bottle of whisky; his wife said he always accused her of drinking it – so she'd prove him right, she said, by offering up a farewell toast. It was a rare, beautiful day so we were not alone at the top, but sharing the view with other walkers. We invited them to join us, and they did.

We walked over to a sheltered corner just past the cairn, and this is how we said goodbye:

'We did not climb all the way up this hill because we believe you are gone, Bob, but because you are still so much with us ... This place is a place you loved – a place that spoke to your heart ... a place that touched that part of you that lives on and still finds ways to be with us. From this moment on, there will not be a book of remembrance to stand in front of, or a stone and grave to tend and lay our flowers on, but there will be the big bright beautiful world that you loved ... There will be all the things that you cared about, for us to be getting on with, and there will be the lives that you touched rippling out to touch other lives, and in all of that you live on.

'We did not climb all the way up this hill because we believe you are gone, Bob, but because you are still so much with us. We've come here because this is where we'll find you. In the wind that blows and gently touches our spirit ... touches that part of us that will live on, and will always find ways to be with you.'

It's Easter sunrise, and we've gathered here not because we believe Jesus is gone, but because we know he's still so much with us. In every decision we make, in every life we touch, in every moment we forgive, he lives on. When we share what we have, when we hold hands with a lover or reach out to a stranger, we celebrate the eternal nature of Jesus Christ.

In our story this morning, the angel told the women: *'Tell his friends that he'll meet them in Galilee.'* He told them to go home; to go back to their lives and live differently.

So this morning, like the wise men at the beginning and the disciples at the end, we go home a different way. And never look back. Amen

AFTER THESE THINGS

(Reflection and meditation)

'After these things, Jesus showed himself again to the disciples by the Sea of Tiberias; and he showed himself in this way.' (John 21:1)

'He showed himself again to his disciples; and he showed himself in this way' ...

Is there more to this than an ancient account most often used as proof of the physical resurrection? Something deeply symbolic, something foundational? Something his disciples needed to understand at the *core* of their beings if they were really to be the ones who would follow in his footsteps; if they were really going to have the courage and patience and wisdom to forge new roads for him? ... Is there something that *we* need to understand at the core of our beings, all these generations past?

'He showed himself again to his disciples; and he showed himself in this way' ...

Is that his plan all along: to show himself again and again and again, in a myriad of faces, in a symphony of voices? Is that his plan all along: to keep on coming – bursting into our lives with an in-your-face 'Here I am – what are you going to do about it?'; or slipping in so quietly that we don't even notice him, until he taps us on the shoulder and gives us that shy uncertain smile? Is that his plan all along – to inject himself into everyone and everything; to keep showing himself to those who want to follow?

Do you hear echoes of that in other stories and sayings, laying the groundwork, opening our eyes and ears, preparing us to take this continuous, essential step?: *'If you do this to the least of these, you do it to me ... Love the*

Lord your God with all your heart and soul, mind and strength, and love your neighbour as much as you love yourself … See, I am with you always, even until the end of the age … Feed my sheep … Follow me.'

There have been times in my life when I *knew* Jesus Christ was standing right in front of me …

He stands in front of us embodied in the people we cannot abide, the ones who have wounded or hurt us, and asks us to be forgiving.

He stands in the shoes of those we would call 'enemy', and says 'I am your brother'.

He stands in front of us with empty eyes – ones that reflect empty stomachs and hopes. When I see images of Darfur, when I think back to Hurricane Katrina, I realise that all those suffering brothers and sisters are Jesus.

'After these things, Jesus showed himself again to the disciples by the Sea of Tiberias; and he showed himself in this way.'

Is there more to this than an ancient account most often used as proof of the physical resurrection? Something deeply symbolic, something foundational? Something his disciples needed to understand at the *core* of their beings if they were really to be the ones who would follow in his footsteps; if they were really going to have the courage and patience and wisdom to forge new roads for him? I think so … And I pray that we, his followers today, have the courage to see.

Think of a time when Jesus stood in front of you. In that moment, what did he need? What did he get? What can you do differently? What did you do well? …

RESURRECTION STORIES

Narrator:

I want you to listen to a story: a pretty hard-to-believe, unlikely story. Some people have difficulty believing it to be true. Others say it is no more than an idle tale.

Reading: Luke 24:1–12

Narrator:

Here are some other stories now. You might be one of those who think they also are hard to believe.

Reading: Luke 8:40–42, 49–55

A young girl:

When folk first heard what he did for me, most thought it was an idle tale. The mourners at our gate even stopped their weeping to laugh and mock him when he said I was only sleeping. They thought I was dead, you know. I'd been so sick for so long that everyone said there was no hope for me. I lived from my bed and listened to whispers:

'What a shame.' 'Poor little lamb.' 'It's God's will.'

But it seems this Jesus had other plans for me: he was a man of life, not death. He took me by the hand and told me to get up, to eat, to live. And I did! And here I am to tell the tale. Who knows what my life will be?

It's a great adventure and it's a gift. I can tell you one thing though: I won't waste it or take it for granted. And I'll always thank God for it because life is God's will. Jesus gave me my life back, so when I heard the 'tale' about him, I wasn't so doubtful, because I guess I was kind of resurrected too.

Reading: John 8:1–11

A woman:

If I'd heard the story of what he did for me, I'd have thought it was an idle tale. Things like that just don't happen in the real world. I'd been caught red-handed, as it were, and the fact that it takes two to tango didn't seem to matter to the crowd at the Temple – especially to the 'holy men'.

This Jesus was teaching a crowd. Everyone was listening to him, and I think that's what had put the scribes and Pharisees in such a foul mood. They were out for blood, and if they couldn't have his, mine would do. I don't know who thought of it first, but I heard them whispering amongst themselves: 'Take her to him.' 'Let's see him get out of this one.' 'Let's see what his God's will would be.' So they made me stand in front of all those people and they humiliated me. I was made to feel subhuman.

They asked him what should be done with me. Should I be stoned, as the Law of Moses calls for? There was silence: he said nothing. Then he just bent down and drew in the sand. You could have heard a pin drop.

Just as the silence was becoming unbearable, he stood up and said it. You know the words … you've heard my story: 'Let anyone of you who is without sin be the very first to throw a stone at her.' And then it happened. They simply walked away: every single one of them, until I was the only one left. I just stood there. I waited. I needed something more, and he gave it to me.

'Has no one condemned you?' he asked.

'No one, sir,' I replied.

'Well then, neither do I. Go and sin no more.'

He gave me my life back, so when I heard the 'tale' about him, I wasn't so doubtful, because, you know this? I was resurrected too.

Reading: Matthew 19:16–22

A young man:

When folk hear what he said to me, most of them think that I was one of his rare failures. They think he didn't convince me or change me or save me. And I can understand that because, you see, I walked away. I couldn't handle what he had to say, what he asked me to do.

I'd been a good Jew all my life: I followed all the rules as best I could. And I studied, and I listened. That's why I went to him in the first place. I'd been listening to him and I was intrigued by what I heard. I suppose I wanted to know what he thought of me.

Maybe deep down I wanted him to tell me that I'd made it: that there wasn't anything else for me to do. But he saw straight through me. 'If you wish to be perfect, go and sell all your possessions. Give the money to the poor and then you will have treasure in heaven. And then after that come and follow me.'

Talk about taking the wind out of your sails! I'm a rich man. I have a lot of things. So I walked away. I couldn't handle what he had to say, what he asked me to do. So folk think I was one of his rare failures … that he didn't convince me or change me or save me.

Now, I can understand that, but there's a little point everyone seems to miss in my story. I went away right enough, but I went away grieving. And the grieving was the beginning of a change. It has taken some time, but I'm becoming convinced. I'm changing, and he did save me. Jesus showed me what life is really about. So when I heard the 'tale' about him, I wasn't so doubtful, because I guess I'm kind of being resurrected too.

SONGBOOKS

CH4 (Church Hymnary 4), Canterbury Press

Common Ground: A Song Book for all the Churches, St Andrew Press

Enemy of Apathy: Songs and Chants for Lent, Eastertide and Pentecost, John L. Bell and Graham Maule, Wild Goose Publications

One Is the Body: Songs of Unity & Diversity, John L. Bell, Wild Goose Publications

Songs of God's People, Oxford University Press

There Is One Among Us: Shorter Songs for Worship, John L. Bell, Wild Goose Publications

SOURCES & ACKNOWLEDGEMENTS

Bible passages from the NRSV. Passages from NRSV copyright 1989, Division of Christian Education of the National Council of the Churches of Christ in the United States of America. Used by permission. All rights reserved.